SOVIET
‹GEORGIA›

SOVIET GEORGIA

Michael Boyette and Randi Boyette

CHELSEA HOUSE PUBLISHERS
New York•Philadelphia

Printed and bound in the United States of America

3 5 7 9 8 6 4 2

Editorial Director: Rebecca Stefoff
Editor: Rafaela Ellis
Copy Editor: Crystal G. Norris
Series Designer: Anita Noble
Designer: A. C. Simon
Production Manager: Les Kaplan
Production Assistant: Victor Rangel-Ribeiro
Photo Researcher: Marty Baldessari

Library of Congress Cataloging-in-Publication Data

Boyette, Randi.
Soviet Georgia.

Includes index.
Summary: Surveys the history, topography, people,
and culture of Soviet Georgia, with an emphasis on its
current economy, industry, and place in the political
world.
1. Georgian S.S.R.—Juvenile literature.
[1. Georgian S.S.R.] I. Boyette, Michael. II. Title.
DK511.G3B69   1988   947'.95   87-18304
ISBN 1-55546-779-2

14.95

‹CONTENTS›

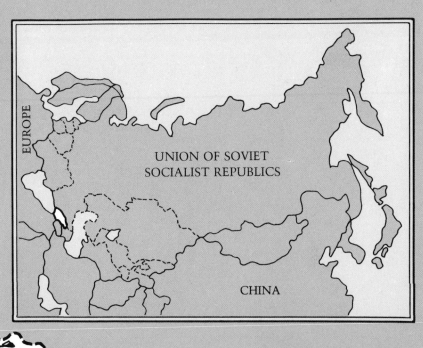

UNION OF SOVIET
SOCIALIST REPUBLICS

EUROPE

CHINA

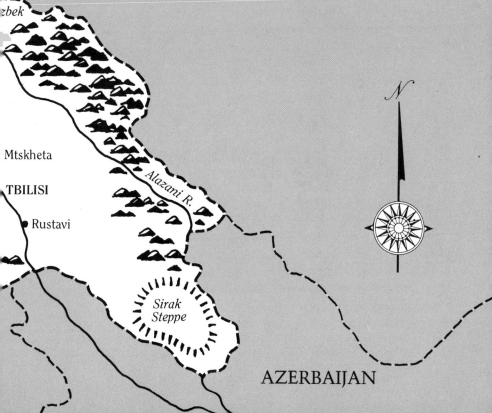

zbek

Mtskheta

TBILISI

Rustavi

Alazani R.

Sirak
Steppe

N

AZERBAIJAN

◄ FACTS AT A GLANCE ►

Land and People

Location	1,000 miles (1600 kilometers) south of Moscow, in the southernmost region of the European section of the USSR
Area	26,911 square miles (69,700 square kilometers)
Highest Point	Shkhara 17,063 feet (5,630 meters)
Major Rivers	Kura, Rioni
Climate	Average temperature in coastal area is about 41° Fahrenheit (5° Centigrade); in eastern lowlands, temperatures range from 32° to 77° F
Annual Rainfall	As little as 16 inches (406 millimeters) in plains and foothills of eastern Georgia; as much as 100 inches (2,540 mm) in coastal areas near the Black Sea
Capital	Tbilisi (population 1,200,000)
Other Major Cities	Kutaisi (population 207,000); Rustavi (population 139,000); Batumi (population 129,000); Sukhumi (population 122,000)
Population	5,203,000
Population Density	193 people per square mile (75 per sq. km.); one of the most densely populated of the Soviet republics
Population Distribution	About 90 percent of population lives at altitudes below 3,300 feet (1,000 meters); density decreases sharply with increasing altitude

Languages	Georgian and Abkhazian are the main languages, but 60 others are spoken
Ethnic Groups	Georgians, 68.8 percent; Armenians, 9 percent; Russians, 7.4 percent; Azerbaijanis, 5.1 percent; Ossetians, 3.2 percent; Abkhazians, 1.7 percent; and smaller numbers of other groups
Religions	Georgian Orthodox (Christian), Muslim, Jewish

Economy

Major Resources	Coal, manganese, hydroelectric power
Major Products	Wines, tea, sheet iron, seamless pipe products
Agricultural Land Use	696 collective farms occupy more than 66 percent of agricultural land; 546 state farms comprise just under 34 percent
Currency	Ruble, equal to about U.S. $1.30
Estimated Annual Government Spending	3,086 million rubles (U.S. $4,011.8 million)
Percentage of National Income	Industry, 39 percent; agriculture, 34.7 percent; construction, 10.9 percent; other, 15.4 percent

Government

Form of government	Socialist republic controlled by the Communist party of the Soviet Union
Georgian Leaders	Chairman, Presidium of the Georgian Supreme Soviet; First Secretary of the Communist party
Eligibility to Vote	All citizens of the USSR who have reached the age of 18

◄HISTORY AT A GLANCE►

30,000 to 10,000 B.C.	The area's earliest societies evolve from nomadic hunter-gatherers to settled tribes engaged in agriculture and cattle raising.
3000 B.C.	Georgia's Bronze Age begins. Metal tools replace crude stone implements.
2000 to 1000 B.C.	The Kartvelian people (ancestors of modern Georgians) form subgroups, each with its own language.
1000 to 100 B.C.	Tribes band together to wage war against their neighbors, leading to the formation of the Colchian and Iberian kingdoms. Greek trading colonies are established on the Black Sea coast.
around 100 B.C.	Rome conquers parts of Georgia.
330 A.D.	Georgia embraces Christianity after St. Nino converts Queen Nana and King Mirian.
330 to 490	The Byzantine and Persian empires fight for control of Georgia.
around 490	King Vakhtang Gorgaslani restores Georgian independence by unifying the many small groups and tribes into one nation. A national language and religion develop.
523	Persians abolish royal government.
523 to around 790	Georgia is ruled by a succession of foreign powers—Persia, Byzantium, and Arab caliphs.
975 to 1014	King Bagrot III unites the Georgian principalities and founds the Bagratid royal house.

around 1000	Turks overrun Georgia and ravage the land.
1089 to 1125	King David II reigns as ruler of Georgian principalities from the Black Sea to the Caspian Sea. It is the beginning of Georgia's Golden Age.
1184 to 1213	Queen Tamara reigns. The boundaries of the kingdom are enlarged and the Golden Age reaches its peak. Shota Rustaveli writes *The Knight in the Tiger's Skin* and dedicates it to Queen Tamara.
1220	Mongols invade Georgia, ending the Golden Age.
1220 to 1314	Mongols rule eastern Georgia; the Bagratid dynasty rule western Georgia.
1314 to 1346	King Giorgi V reigns after the Mongol withdrawal.
1366	The Black Death (bubonic plague) strikes Georgia.
1386 to 1403	New invasions of Mongols reduce the country to ruins.
1412 to 1443	Reign of Alexander I, the last king of united Georgia.
1443 to 1783	Control goes back and forth between Turks and Persians, who divide the country and prevent the development of a strong independent government.
1783	Erekle II, ruler of Kartalinia and the Kakhetian states, turns to Catherine the Great of Russia for aid; the Treaty of Georgievsk results.
1795	The treaty proves worthless as Persians attack Tbilisi.
1801 to 1878	Russia annexes Georgian kingdoms one by one, and regains control of Turkish-dominated Black Sea ports and areas of southwestern Georgia.

1864	Serfdom is abolished in Georgia.
around 1880	Resistance to Russian rule grows.
1893	Noë Zhordania leads the founding of the Social Democratic party in Georgia.
1905 to 1917	Revolution rocks Russia. Georgia's Social Democrats gain in strength and number.
March 1917	The Russian Empire crumbles. The Kerensky government (a provisional revolutionary government) takes power temporarily, but major disagreements erupt between the Bolsheviks and the Mensheviks. Georgia is governed by a Kerensky-appointed committee.
October 1917	Bolsheviks under Vladimir Lenin gain power in Russia. Menshevik-dominated Georgia, Armenia, and Azerbaijan form the Transcaucasian Commissariat.
April 1918	In spite of ongoing peace negotiations, Turkey invades the Georgian city of Batumi.
May 1918	Georgia declares its independence as the Georgian Social Democratic Republic and places itself under the protection of Imperial Germany.
November 1918	Germany surrenders, leading to British occupation of Georgia.
1920	The British leave Georgia.
1922 to 1924	Georgian nationalists resist Soviet control and repression. When revolt finally breaks out, Red Army troops quickly defeat it.
December 1936	The Transcaucasian Soviet Federated Socialist Republic is dissolved. The Georgian Soviet Socialist Republic becomes one of 15 republics of the USSR.
1936 to present	Under Soviet power, Georgia is transformed into a modern industrial society.

The mountains of the Caucasus are dotted with remote and fairly inaccessible settlements, such as this one at Trishetiya.

Soviet Georgia and the World

The great land masses of Asia and Europe meet on a strip of land known as Transcaucasia, an isolated region located between the Black Sea and the Caspian Sea. Transcaucasia is bounded to the north and the south by the rugged Caucasus mountains. Nestled in this mountainous area is Soviet Georgia. Its full name is the Georgian Soviet Socialist Republic and it is one of the 15 republics that make up the Union of Soviet Socialist Republics (USSR), or, as it is often called, the Soviet Union.

Because of its location, Soviet Georgia has been influenced by both Europe and Asia. But the tiny republic's history and the ethnic identity of its people are unique. For more than 2,000 years Georgia suffered almost continuous invasions and occupations by European and Asian armies, but its people kept their independent spirit and culture alive. Today, as part of the Soviet Union, Georgia retains its special character and plays an important role in the politics and economy of the country.

Soviet Georgia is a major source of raw manufacturing materials for the Soviet Union. Iron ore and manganese are mined from its rich earth and processed in its steel mills. Georgia's chemical industry gives the nation fertilizers, synthetic materials, and medica-

Pitsunda, the ancient Greek colony of Pitiunt, is one of the most popular resorts on the Black Sea.

tions, and its modern factories make products that range from heavy farm equipment to light silk fabric.

The Soviet Union also looks to Georgia for agricultural products. Georgia's more than 70 tea factories provide 95 percent of the tea produced in the Soviet Union. Its vine-growing countryside produces grapes for table and dessert wines, some of which have won international awards. Its fields and orchards also yield tobacco, fruit, and flowers.

Georgia's breathtaking landscapes vary from subtropical Black Sea shores to snow-capped mountain peaks. The Caucasus Mountains form a barrier that protects the republic from the frigid temperatures so common in the northern and central parts of the Soviet Union. The capital city, Tbilisi, has a distinctly Mediterranean flavor, with gardens and tile-roofed houses.

Georgia's population is diverse and includes city dwellers and villagers, farmers and factory workers. Despite their differences, the various ethnic groups get along with one another. Perhaps they are bound together by a shared history of having been conquered by powerful neighbors. Perhaps the centuries have simply taught them to live together in harmony.

Although Soviet Georgia is part of a world superpower, it is far removed from Soviet politics. It is a rich and varied republic, but its small size, remote location, and the difficulty of its language make it a mysterious place in the eyes of most Westerners.

In Tbilisi, the capital of Soviet Georgia, narrow streets crowd pedestrians and vehicles.

A Corner
of Paradise

Georgians like to tell a story about their homeland: On the eighth day of creation, God gave land to the many peoples of the earth. When he had finished, he started for home and met the Georgians sitting at a table along the roadside. God said, "While I was dividing up the world, you just sat here, eating and drinking wine. Now there's no land left for you."

"That may be so," replied one of the Georgians, "but while you were busy, we didn't forget you. We drank many toasts to you, thanking you for such a beautiful world."

"That's more than anyone else did," said God. "And so I'm going to give you the last little corner of the world—the part that I was saving for myself because it is so much like paradise."

Georgians have good reason to appreciate their country's geography. The land is rich and varied, with towering mountains and fertile lowlands. To the north lies the rugged Caucasus mountain range—a land of glaciers, ice, and snow. In the center of the region the mountains give way to high plains, an extension of the central Asian steppes (vast expanses of land that are covered with sparse vegetation). In the west is Georgia's Black Sea coast, with a geography and climate like those of Greece and Turkey. This semitropical coastal area boasts some of the most fertile and productive farmland in the Soviet Union. Along the southern border, another range of mountains called the Lower Caucasus (also the Lesser Caucasus) separates Georgia from Turkey.

Surprisingly, all of this variety is contained in a fairly small area. The total area of the Georgian Soviet Socialist Republic is only 26,911 square miles (69,700 square kilometers), which makes the republic a little smaller than the state of South Carolina.

Georgia itself is one of 15 republics that make up the USSR. The largest Soviet republic is the Russian Soviet Federated Socialist Republic, or Russia. It bounds Georgia to the north of the Caucasus Mountains. Two small Soviet republics, the Azerbaijan Soviet Socialist Republic (Azerbaijan) and the Armenian Soviet Socialist Republic (Armenia), border Georgia on the southeast. Along with Soviet Georgia, these two Soviet republics make up the area known as Transcaucasia.

The republic of Georgia itself includes the Abkhazian Autonomous Soviet Socialist Republic (Abkhazia), the Adzharian Autonomous Soviet Socialist Republic (Adzharia), and the South Ossetian Autonomous Oblast (an oblast is a region set aside within the Soviet Union for a small ethnic population). Each of these areas is the homeland within Georgia of an ethnic group. Abkhazia's and Adzharia's populations are large enough to make them autonomous republics, which means these two areas have their own state governments and constitutions. South Ossetia does not have this control over local government because its population is so small. All these areas have limited rights and are under the supervision of the Soviet Georgian government.

Much of Georgia is covered by the Caucasus mountain range (called Kavkasioni in Georgian), which is one of the highest mountain ranges in the world. Many of its peaks are equal to those of the Alps or the Rockies. Most of the Caucasus is from 9,000 to 12,000

In the foothills of the Caucasus Mountains, women tend vines at the Manavy State Farm.

feet (2,743 and 3,658 meters) above sea level. Georgia's highest peaks are Shkhara, at 17,063 feet (5,630 m), Dzhangitau, at 16,565 feet (5,466 m), and Kazbek, at 16,558 feet (5,464 m). Mount Elbrus, just north of the republic's border, is the highest peak in Europe at 18,510 feet (5,642 m).

One of the most famous myths of ancient Greece is set on the slopes of Mount Elbrus. According to the myth, Zeus, the king of the gods, chained the warrior Prometheus to a rock on the mountainside after he stole the secret of fire and brought it to mankind. The Georgians have made good use of his gift. For thousands of

years, their forges have produced richly worked bronze and other metals, earning Georgians wide recognition as talented metalworkers.

Today, the mountains that supplied the ancient Georgians with ore for metalworking provide the Soviet Union with raw materials, such as coal and manganese (a metal used to make high-grade steel). The people still take pride in their traditional metalworking skills,

The rugged beauty of much of Georgia is shown in this view of the Voenno-Gruzenska Road through Mount Kasbek.

but Georgia now boasts modern factories that manufacture everything from heavy farm equipment to airplanes. The power to run these factories comes from more than 200 hydroelectric dams on Georgia's fast-flowing rivers.

The climate in the mountains—especially the western slopes that receive rain from the Black Sea—favors many kinds of crops, including wheat, barley, oats, peaches, apples, cherries, apricots, and plums. In addition, shepherds in the mountain *auls* (villages) raise sheep and goats. The scenery and cool weather make the mountains a popular area for skiing, climbing, or boating on the many lakes.

Much of the mountainous countryside is still wild. Oak and beech trees cover the lower slopes. Forests of Caucasian fir and spruce grow higher up. As one ascends, these trees give way to birch, juniper, and thickets of rhododendrons and azaleas, then to alpine meadows, and finally to rocks and ice. Bears, wolves, wildcats, foxes, and other forms of wildlife abound in the mountains.

In the central eastern part of Georgia, between the northern and southern mountain ranges, stands the high rolling country around Tbilisi, the capital. Mountains separate the humid coastal area from this region, which receives relatively little rainfall—less than 20 inches (508 millimeters) per year on the average. This warm, dry countryside is ideal for growing grapes, and Georgian wine from this area is considered to be among the finest wines in the Soviet Union. Large irrigation projects have also made it possible to grow other crops, such as winter wheat.

Through this region runs the Kura River, Georgia's longest. The Kura begins about 100 miles (160 kilometers) from the Black Sea, in the mountains of Turkey. The mountains, however, force it east, away from the Black Sea and into the interior of Georgia. The river flows past Gori, the birthplace of Soviet dictator Joseph Stalin, and Mtskheta, Georgia's ancient capital, where sheep now graze among historic forts and churches. A little farther on, the Kura passes beneath the high bluffs of Tbilisi and then heads south-east toward Azerbaijan. The Kura River finally empties into the Caspian Sea, about 500 miles (800 km) from its source.

To the west of Tbilisi, the Suram Mountains run north and south, separating the warm, dry lands of the east from the coastal region of the Black Sea. Like Tbilisi and the Caucasus, the Black Sea coast of Georgia is steeped in legend. According to Greek mythology, Jason and the Argonauts sought the Golden Fleece in this low-lying area called Kolkhida, or Colchis. The main city of the area, Sukhumi, claims to trace its ancestry to Castor and Pollux, the mythical Greek twins known as the Gemini, who traveled here with Jason.

The Georgian coastline does yield wealth, although not from the Golden Fleece. Its wealth comes from the land itself. In fact, this area is the most fertile in all of the Soviet Union. The climate is warm, the days are long, and the annual rainfall averages more than 40 inches (1,016 millimeters). Some parts of this region are swampy and thinly settled, the haunts of huge flocks of ducks and other water birds.

A country of legends, beauty, and history, Soviet Georgia is truly an enchanted land. The republic's remarkable variety of landscapes— from soaring mountains to the Black Sea coast—makes it easy to see why Georgians believe they live in a tiny corner of paradise.

Demonstrators at a street rally in Tbilisi welcome former Soviet Premier Brezhnev during a visit.

The People of Soviet Georgia

Georgia and the people who live there are known by many names. The Georgians call themselves "Kartelebi" and their homeland "Sakartvelos." The European name "Georgia" (called "Gruziya" in Russian) comes from the Arabic and Persian name of the region, "Gurjistan." This, in turn, is related to the Syrian "Gurzan" and the Middle Persian "Wyrshn."

Georgia's people are diverse. There are Christians, Muslims and Jews; city dwellers and villagers; factory workers and shepherds. As a people, Georgians are noted for their bravery, warmth, and generosity.

The government, not individual citizens, owns and controls most businesses in the USSR. But the people of Soviet Georgia have not forgotten their heritage as a nation of traders. According to a Georgian saying, it may be a crime to be rich in a Socialist country, but in Georgia it is also a disgrace to be poor. Georgians want to give their children the best in life, and they strive to live as well as or better than their neighbors. Many Georgians do, in fact, have a higher standard of living than citizens of other Soviet republics.

Through the ages, Georgians have been known for their excellence as warriors, marksmen, horsemen, herdsmen, and winemakers. Today, a large number of the Soviet Union's professors, doctors, teachers, civil servants, artists, and army officers come from Georgia. In fact, Georgians have contributed far more to the Soviet Union's intellectual life than one might expect from a small outlying republic.

Georgians are very proud of the customs and the language of their republic. In 1977, for example, students at the University of Tbilisi risked arrest and prison sentences when they demonstrated to keep Georgian the official language. Georgia has been an important part of the Soviet Union for more than 60 years, but nationalist sentiment—love of Georgia's own characteristics and history apart from those of the Soviet Union—still runs high. These feelings of nationalism have sometimes taken the form of movements in favor of Georgian independence.

Georgians are also famous for their hospitality and joy of life. They love to celebrate with vigorous dancing, good food, and wine. Birthdays, especially those marking the end of a decade, are celebrated with huge parties. Weddings are joyous events, whether a couple is married in business clothes at the local government office or in traditional costumes in a religious ceremony. In addition to religious holidays, most Georgians celebrate a traditional Georgian holiday known as the Festival of the Grape Harvest, or Rtveli. Georgians also celebrate government holidays, such as November 7 (in honor of the 1917 October Revolution), May Day, Soviet Constitution Day (October 7), Victory Day (May 9), and International Women's Day (March 8).

These celebrations feature some of the most delicious and interesting foods in the Soviet Union. Georgian cooking resembles that of the Middle East and uses seasonings like paprika, cayenne, ginger, sesame seeds, garlic, mint, and coriander.

One well-known Georgian dish is *shashlyk*. Similar to a shish kebab, it includes lamb and onions roasted on a skewer—or in days past, on a bayonet thrust into the campfire. Chicken *tabaka* (chicken coated with bread crumbs), *khachapuri* (cheese pie), and *suluguni* (goat cheese) are other regional favorites.

Most Georgians dress like Americans or Europeans, but some of them occasionally wear the traditional *cherkeska* (knee-length tunic) with soft, high boots and a *burkah* (cape) flung over the shoulders. In the mountains, some men even sport daggers on their belts and silver-clasped cartridge cases on their chests. Women also may be seen wearing cherkeskas, although theirs are decorated with etched silver chains and buckles. Many farm women still cover their heads with headscarves.

Bending the Rules

The Georgians tend to be individualistic and exuberant. Yet they live under a Communist system of government that stresses order, planning, and collective work. In order to live under this system, Georgians sometimes have to bend the rules. They even have a special term, *blat,* for all the ways of getting around the rules and regulations to meet the needs that the Soviet economy neglects. Blat (obtaining jobs or other benefits through personal favors and personal influence, rather than by merit) extends from the practice of patronage to outright fraud.

Because of their blat activities, the Georgians have earned a reputation as black-market traders. An example of this spirit is the Georgian practice of taking cheap airline flights to Moscow to sell flowers. Flowers are in great demand in the Soviet Union and are a very profitable commodity. And in Georgia's warm climate, flowers are easy to grow. So in spite of official disapproval, Georgians often fly north with suitcases full of flowers to sell in northern cities.

In fact, Georgians tell a joke about the hijacking of an airplane on its way from Georgia to Moscow. When the hijackers ordered the pilot to fly to Paris, they were overpowered by Georgian passengers,

A Georgian couple shops for bread at a small local grocery.

who told the pilot to fly on to Moscow. When the plane landed, the Georgians were greeted as heroes. A friend took them aside and asked them why they risked their lives when they could have done nothing and gone to Paris. They replied, "But what would we have done with 2,000 daffodils in Paris?"

Because of their long, friendly bond with the Russians, the Soviet Union's largest ethnic group, Georgians have enjoyed a special place in Soviet politics. Until recently, they were allowed to bend the rules somewhat in running their own government. But in 1973, a Georgian named Otari Lazeifvili took blat a bit too far, and created a national scandal. He was accused of pocketing a million rubles that should have gone to the government. Some Georgians took a strange sort of pride in him, bragging that the amount was really much greater and relishing the accounts of his numerous underground (unofficial) factories, which manufactured clothes to sell on the black market. The Soviet government has tightened its control over Georgian affairs since the Lazeifvili affair. But many Georgians still chuckle when they tell Lazeifvili's story.

A Land of Many Peoples

Native Georgians comprise nearly 69 percent of the 5.2 million inhabitants of Soviet Georgia. They are divided into many subgroups, each with its own dialects and customs. Many trace their ancestry to the various traders, invaders, and refugees that settled in Georgia's cities and isolated mountain regions. Other peoples who live in Georgia include Armenians, Russians, Azerbaijans, Ossets, Greeks, Abkhazians, Ukranians, Jews, Kurds, Tatars, Byelorussians, and Assyrians.

As early as the 1st century, the Romans at Dioscurias (a trading colony on Georgia's Black Sea coast) reportedly needed interpreters for 130 languages. Even today, about 60 languages are still spoken in addition to the two main ones, Georgian and Abkhazian.

The Abkhazians are a particularly visible minority because they inhabit their own separate republic within Georgia, the Abkhazian Autonomous Soviet Socialist Republic. This unique territory has its own government and language. The Abkhazians are mostly mountain people, and their primary occupation is sheepherding. There are more centenarians (people more than 100 years old) in Abkhazia than anywhere else in the Soviet Union.

One of Georgia's mountain tribes is the Khevsurs, who are said to be the bravest people in the Caucasus. The Khevsurs claim to be descended from soldiers of the Crusades who settled in Georgia rather than returning to Europe. In fact, some linguists (scientists who study language) have traced Khevsurian names back to Hungarian roots. Today the Khevsurs are mostly shepherds on collective, or group-owned, farms. On feast days the Khevsurs still wear their

The Muslim presence throughout the Soviet republics in the south is evident in this group of mullahs at the mosque of Azizy near Batum.

traditional chain mail (flexible armor of linked metal rings) marked with Maltese crosses.

In other deep mountain valleys are remnants of once-fierce tribes, such as the Chechen, Ingushi, and Kabardian. Some of these groups resisted Soviet rule during World War II. Stalin, who believed that they had helped the Germans, ordered them deported to Siberia after the war ended. They remained in exile until after he died.

The Muslim population of Georgia is centered in Batumi. This is the capital of the Adzharian Autonomous Soviet Socialist Republic. Ossets living in the South Ossetian Autonomous Oblast are descendants of the people driven across the Caucasus Mountains by the Mongols in the 13th century.

Georgia's Jewish population includes the Judeo-Tats (mountain Jews), who live in mountain valleys. There are reports of people of

African descent also living in the mountains. These people may be the descendants of slaves who were brought to Georgia centuries ago.

The Georgian Church

The Soviet government officially discourages the nation's citizens from practicing any religion, at times persecuting or denying privileges to those who continue to practice their beliefs. Soviet newspapers report a steady decline in the number of believers nationwide, but not in Soviet Georgia. The Georgian church remains a powerful force in the lives of many people, despite the changes the Soviet government has forced on it. In recent years, the Georgians have restored many of the old stone houses of worship and have reopened some of them for services.

The governments of Georgia and neighboring Armenia show greater tolerance toward religion than do most Soviet republics, because the Georgian and Armenian churches are national churches. This means that, unlike religions such as Catholicism and Islam, they do not look to leaders in other nations for guidance. Georgia's national faith is related to the Greek Orthodox form of Christianity.

The center of Georgian Orthodoxy is a church called Sveti Tskhoveli (Pillar of Life) in Mtskheta, Georgia's ancient capital. According to a local legend, a merchant brought the robe of Christ to Mtskheta. When his daughter died, he buried her in it, and in that spot a grove of cedars sprang up. Those cedars were then used to build the first church in Georgia during the 4th century. In the 5th century, the church was rebuilt with stone; in the 11th century, Sveti Tskhoveli was built around it. From the 5th century A.D. until 1812, Georgian kings and queens were crowned and buried in this church.

Like most Georgian churches, Sveti Tskhoveli is capped by a low tower and a pointed cupola (domelike structure). Its walls are

This elderly man is typical of the many long-lived Georgians of popular imagination.

150 feet (45 meters) high and up to 75 feet (23 m) thick. It is still in use, and on Sundays hundreds of people gather to worship among the tombs of the ancient rulers of their land.

Georgia's Centenarians

The Georgians, along with their neighbors, the Armenians and the Azerbaijanians, live an unusually long time. According to the Soviet government, 39 out of every 100,000 Georgians live past age 100.

These centenarians are called *dolgozhiteli,* and the Soviet national newspaper, *Pravda,* regularly publishes photos of them.

Most centenarians live full lives, often working and relaxing as young persons might. They believe their good health and long lives come from hard work and a diet that mainly consists of vegetables, kefir (a liquid yogurt), and other dairy products. Reportedly, they also rise early, drink natural spring water and tea, bathe in cold river water, and occasionally fast to rest their stomachs.

A chalice cover, in the form of a Greek cross, is made of linen embroidered in metal thread and colored silk.

Soviet Georgia's Troubled History

Since the Stone Age, people have lived in the region that is now Soviet Georgia. Many ancient sites and monuments have been discovered and excavated in the republic, mainly in the Rioni River valley and on the seaboard of Abkhazia. These archaeological finds show how early human society progressed from bands of hunters moving through the countryside in search of food to more settled communities of people who farmed and raised livestock.

About 2000 B.C., the ancestors of modern Georgians called themselves the Kartvelians. They were divided into three main subgroups, each with its own language: the Iberians, the Svans, and the Mingrelo-Laz. The Mingrelo-Laz lived along the Black Sea coast, the Svans formed independent tribes in the mountain valleys, and the Iberians dominated the rest of the region.

Around 1000 B.C., society started to change. The peoples living in Georgia banded together to wage war against their neighbors. They built fortresses and carved out states and kingdoms. Greek explorers established trading colonies on the Black Sea coast, including Phasis and Dioscurias. Two main kingdoms formed: the Colchian Kingdom along the coast and the Kartlian, or Iberian, Kingdom in what is now eastern Georgia.

In the 1st century B.C., the Romans tried to conquer the country. For a time, the Romans directly ruled Colchis and managed to exert some control over Iberia, but their power over the area soon declined.

Perhaps the most important event in early Georgian history was the conversion of the people to Christianity. In the 4th century A.D., St. Nino, a slave woman said to have healing powers, brought Christianity to Georgia. St. Nino converted Queen Nana to the faith by displaying her powers. King Mirian converted after seeing a solar eclipse. The people of the land soon followed the monarchs' example, embracing Christianity and becoming strong believers.

After Georgia's conversion to Christianity, the Byzantine and Persian empires fought for control of the land. Toward the end of the 5th century, King Vakhtang Gorgaslani won Georgia's independence. Georgians continue to tell stories of the king's wisdom and bravery.

Under the kings that followed Gorgaslani, the many small groups and tribes that lived in the region slowly united into one nation. A national language and religion developed, as did Georgian forms of culture, such as distinctive dress, weapons, and utensils. However, foreign powers continued to dominate Georgia, except for brief periods of national independence.

In 523 A.D., the Persians abolished the Georgian royal government. For the next three centuries, Georgia was ruled, first by Persia (modern-day Iran), and then by Byzantium (modern-day Turkey). After 654 A.D., Muslim Arabs ruled Georgia.

For hundreds of years, life in Georgia was feudal. The common people were enslaved by the nobles, who in turn banded together into a number of principalities (small independent states). King Bagrat III, who reigned from 975 to 1014, united these principalities into a single feudal state, although Tbilisi remained under Muslim rule.

Soon after 1000 A.D., Turks from the south overran Georgia. For more than 20 years, the invaders ravaged the land without mercy. King David II, known as David the Restorer or David the Builder, came to the Georgian throne in 1089, just as the power of the Turks was decreasing. He took advantage of their decline and, by the time of his death in 1125, he ruled over Georgians, Armenians, and Muslims from the Black Sea to the Caspian Sea. He also recaptured Tbilisi from the Arabs. This marked the beginning of Georgia's Golden Age.

The Golden Age

Georgia's Golden Age reached its peak in the 12th century, during the reign of Queen Tamara, the great-granddaughter of David II. When she came to the throne in 1184, she was young and beautiful. As a leader, she was said to be wise, gentle, and brave. Georgia's

Genghis Khan's son and successor, Ogadai, is depicted in this painting on silk.

most famous literary work, *The Knight in the Tiger's Skin,* was dedicated to her by its author, the 12th-century poet Shota Rustaveli.

By the time Queen Tamara died in 1213, she had secured for herself a place of honor in Georgian history. She had also enlarged the boundaries of the kingdom. Unfortunately, her descendants did not rule as well as she did. Mongols from Asia invaded, ending Geor-

gia's Golden Age and splitting the country in two. The Mongols ruled eastern Georgia, but western Georgia, or Imeretia, remained independent. The Mongols severely punished those who resisted them, but they were lenient to those who accepted their rule.

The Mongols left Georgia to invade other lands in the early 1300s. The nation began to recover during the reign of King Giorgi

This painting shows the surrender of the Georgian leader Shamil to Russian generals in the 19th century.

V (1314 to 1346). But Georgia was soon ravaged again. First the Black Death (bubonic plague) struck in 1366. As Georgia began to recover from that horror, the Mongols returned in 1386 with renewed strength. During the next 17 years, a series of invasions reduced Georgia to ruins.

The last king of united Georgia was Alexander I, who reigned from 1412 until 1443. Under his descendants, the country disintegrated into the small, independent, squabbling kingdoms of Kartalinia, Kakhetia, Imeretia, Guriar, Mingreliar, Svanetiar, and Abkhazia.

For the next 300 years, the Turks and Persians again fought for control of Georgia. Although neither of these southern neighbors could totally dominate Georgia, they did prevent a strong independent government from forming there. Constant war devastated Georgia, and its population was greatly reduced.

The slave trade also plagued Georgia. Georgian women, prized for their dark-eyed beauty, were frequently stolen for the harems of Turkish sultans and Persian shahs. Sometimes they were sold to wealthy Georgians from other tribes.

Slowly, Georgia renewed the ties with Russia that had been severed during the Mongol invasions. It established a Georgian colony in Moscow in the late 17th century, and the rulers of Georgia's independent kingdoms obtained military aid from Russia against the Turks and the Persians.

In the second half of the 18th century, the kingdoms of Kartalinia, Kakhetia, and Imeretia became stronger. The Turks and Persians, however, still threatened Georgia. This led the Georgians of Kartalinia and Kakhetia to look again to Russia for help.

And so a treaty of friendship, called the Treaty of Georgievsk, was drawn up in 1783 by the Kartalinia-Kakhetian king, Erekle II, and the ruler of Russia, Catherine the Great. Under the treaty, Georgia kept its independence in name only and accepted Russia's control over its affairs. Little came of this treaty, however, because the Persians attacked in 1795 and Tbilisi was sacked once more. Erekle II died brokenhearted in 1798. His son, Giorgi XII, tried to hand over the country unconditionally to the Russian tsar (ruler) Paul I, but both rulers died before the plan could be carried out.

Finally, in 1801, Tsar Alexander I of Russia took control of the Kartalinian-Kakhetian state of Georgia. In spite of the treaty of Georgievsk, the tsar removed the Georgian royal family from power and replaced it with Russian military governors.

Russia annexed the other Georgian kingdoms one by one. It added Imeretia in 1810, Guria in 1829, Mingrelia in 1857, Svanetia in 1858, and Abkhazia in 1864. The Black Sea ports of Poti and Batumi, as well as areas of southwestern Georgia that had long been under Turkish rule, came under Russian rule in 1877 and 1878.

Some of the Russian governors behaved so badly that they provoked several uprisings. But many Georgians were grateful to be under the protective wing of the Russians. Life in Georgia became more modern under the tsars. They ordered the construction of highways, railroads, mines, factories, and large plantations to take advantage of the region's wealth. In 1861, Russia abolished serfdom, the feudal system that required peasants to work on the lands of the nobility. Three years later, Georgia also abolished serfdom.

In the 1890s, resistance to Russian rule grew throughout Georgia. The reasons for this unrest included nationalism (the belief that each people should govern themselves) and discontent with low wages and poor working conditions among the growing number of workers in the cities. The tsar's secret police tried unsuccessfully to stamp out the underground (illegal) resistance groups. Some of these groups were attracted to the ideas of Karl Marx, who said that the workers should own and operate the means of production and distribution (farms, factories, and the like). These Georgian groups wanted to set up a "worker's state" based on Marx's ideas.

The most extreme Georgian resistance group was the Social Democratic party, which was founded in 1893 and led by Noë Zhordania. In its ranks was a young Georgian named Joseph Dzhugashvili. He later became Zhordania's rival and, under the revolutionary name of Stalin (man of steel), would rule the Soviet Union with an iron hand for 25 years.

Revolution rocked Russia throughout the first years of the 20th century. The first attempt to overthrow the tsar in 1905 was unsuccessful. In 1917, the revolutionaries finally succeeded. Between 1905 and 1917, the Social Democrats in Georgia gained in strength and numbers, often clashing with Russian soldiers who were loyal to the tsar.

When the Russian revolutionaries won in 1917, the Georgian Social Democrats believed they had a chance to establish a state controlled by the workers—if they could survive long enough. The revolution had come in the midst of World War I, and once again Georgia found itself caught between warring empires.

After the Revolution

When Imperial Russia collapsed, so did its control over its colonies, including Georgia. Georgia suddenly found itself threatened by revolution and by powerful nations beyond its borders. For nearly a decade, Georgia pitted one power against another as it tried to solve its problems and emerge as an independent nation.

Imperial Russia came to an end in March 1917, when Tsar Nicholas II abdicated (gave up control of the government). The revolutionaries formed a temporary government that would hold power only long enough to permit the formation of the Constituent Assembly, a democratically elected body with representatives from all parts of the union. Prince George Lvov was made head of the temporary government.

Tartar prisoners accompany their leader after being captured in battle against the Germans near Tiflis during World War II.

In July, Prince Lvov resigned as head of the government. Aleksander Kerensky took his place. Kerensky could not control Russia, much less Georgia and the other colonies. Throughout the summer of 1917, revolutionary groups fought among themselves, each trying to seize control of the government. The major disagreements took place within the Social Democratic party, which had split into the Bolsheviks (majority) and the Mensheviks (minority) factions (groups) in 1903. Under its leaders Leon Trotsky and Vladimir Lenin, the Bolshevik faction—renamed the Communist party in 1919—called for extreme measures; the Mensheviks wanted to use moderate ones.

Although the fighting between the Mensheviks and Bolsheviks was bloody and bitter in Russia, relations between the two groups were fairly good in Georgia. The Kerensky government appointed a committee, the "Ozakom," to govern Georgia, Azerbaijan, and Armenia. The Ozakom included Mensheviks and Bolsheviks and was led by Mensheviks Noë Zhordania and Noë Ramishvili.

With World War I raging, the Georgian leaders wanted to maintain ties with Russia. They feared they might otherwise be invaded by Turkey, Germany, or some other warring nation. Russia was still at war with the German-Turkish alliance. The Bolsheviks wanted to end the war at any price, but the Georgian Mensheviks wanted to keep fighting to prevent a Turkish invasion.

By the fall of 1917, confusion reigned in Georgia and Russia, and food was scarce. Georgia and its neighbors depended on grain from Russia, but the war meant that little grain was grown and even less of it was distributed to outlying colonies. Tbilisi needed ten wagonloads of wheat a day for its inhabitants, but received only four. City dwellers fled or were evacuated to the countryside, where food was more plentiful. Schools in Tbilisi shut their doors, and students were sent to the country.

In November 1917, the Bolsheviks came to power in Russia, with Lenin acting as chief of state. The Mensheviks who dominated Georgia refused to recognize the Bolsheviks, but they were not willing to declare themselves independent of Russia. Eventually, Georgia and the neighboring regions formed a governmental body called the Transcaucasian Commissariat. It was run by Mensheviks and did not allow Bolshevik members.

In March 1918, the Russian Bolsheviks signed the Treaty of Brest-Litovsk, which ended Russia's participation in World War I. But the Transcaucasian Commissariat refused to honor the treaty, which gave the Black Sea port of Batumi and part of the surrounding Adzharian region of Georgia to the Turks. Encouraged by this confusion in the former Russian Empire, the Turks invaded Batumi and soon occupied nearly all of the territory they wanted.

In April 1918, convinced that the Bolsheviks would retain power in Russia, the Mensheviks announced the creation of an independent state, the Democratic Federative Republic of Transcaucasia, which included Georgia, Azerbaijan and other territories. The new nation lasted just one month. Nationalistic feelings in the various territories, combined with unsuccessful negotiations with Turkey, led the Mensheviks to dissolve the republic on May 24. On May 26, the Georgians declared themselves independent and placed their newly formed Georgian Social Democratic Republic under the protection of Imperial Germany. Knowing that they did not have the power to defend themselves against powerful nations, the Georgians had decided that they would rather be ruled by Christian Germany than by Muslim Turkey or Bolshevik Russia.

After Germany surrendered to Great Britain, France, the United States, and the other nations that opposed it in November 1918, the British occupied Georgia. They restored the Batumi region, which had gone to the Turks under the Brest-Litvosk treaty, to Georgia. The British hoped to restore Imperial Russia. But the Georgian government opposed this plan, and the Georgian people disliked the British presence. The British agreed to withdraw within a year.

Meanwhile, in Russia, civil war was heating up. The Bolsheviks, who were known as the Reds or Communists, were locked in combat with the Whites, a loose collection of groups opposed to communism who hoped to establish a different government in Russia.

The Whites had many competing factions and much disorganization in the top ranks. Many people in Russia and throughout the world supported the Whites in the hopes that they would establish a government more democratic and less extreme than that of the Bolsheviks. But not all of the Whites had democracy in mind. In fact, many simply wanted to restore the old tsarist imperial order.

One of the worst White leaders was General Anton Deniken, who fought primarily in the Caucasus and nearby parts of Russia. In 1919, he blockaded Georgia and Azerbaijan, despite the fact that these regions were anti-Bolshevik like the Whites. He did this because he believed they had "sprung up to the detriment of Russian state interests" and should not receive food "at the expense of the areas of Russia which are being liberated from the Bolsheviks." It is unclear why Deniken blockaded two allies, because Deniken and the Whites needed all the help they could get. Aided by Deniken's poor tactics, the Reds made steady advances.

By July 1920, the Red Army had surrounded Georgia, and the British had withdrawn. Although the people once again proclaimed their independence, they knew that it was only a matter of time before the Reds exerted their control.

After the Bolsheviks' Red Army triumphed over the White Army in 1920, the Bolshevik government named Joseph Stalin commissar of nationalities. Stalin was told to create a plan to deal with Imperial Russia's ex-colonies, including Georgia, his homeland. These colonies presented a problem for the Bolsheviks, who had condemned governments that took over other nations against their wills. How, then, could they reconquer the colonies?

Stalin developed the idea that the former colonies—including Georgia—were free and independent nations. If they wished, they could join Soviet Russia in the Union of Soviet Socialist Republics. The nations could leave the union whenever they wished. But there was a catch: the Soviet government recognized Bolsheviks as the only true representatives of the people and, as such, they were the only group entitled to govern the "independent" republics.

The Red Army forced the Mensheviks who held power in Georgia to come to terms with the Soviet government in Moscow. The Mensheviks agreed to a treaty with Soviet Russia, pledging to expel the White Russian army and all foreign troops. They also agreed to Bolshevik demands that they free Bolshevik political prisoners and not interfere with the party's activities.

The agreement lasted less than a year. The Soviets accused Georgia's Menshevik government of violating the treaty; the Georgian government in turn claimed that the Bolsheviks had sabotaged their government.

(continued on page 57)

SCENES OF
SOVIET
GEORGIA

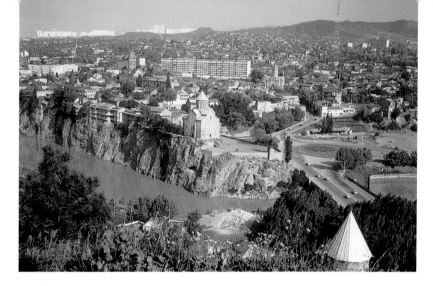

⋀ *Tbilisi, the Georgian capital, has an engaging mixture of traditional and modern architecture.*

➤ *Bathers crowd the beach at a popular Black Sea resort.*

◄ *Like other Soviet cities, Tbilisi mounts a colorful May Day parade and demonstration.*

⋏ *The oil industry is one of the major financial under-pinnings of the Georgian economy.*

◄ *Georgian villages like Mleti are dotted throughout the mountains.*

➤ *Sheep can be raised more readily than cattle on the mountainous slopes of the Caucasus.*

⋎ *The village of Shatili is built around ancient fortifications.*

∧ Khevsuri, one of the
native peoples, cross
their fields in the
Caucasus.

◄ The new sea terminal at
Batumi is deep enough
to accommodate large
tankers and container
ships.

ʌ *Many of the women and girls among the tea pickers are ethnic Greeks.*

‹ *This young woman takes a break from picking tea leaves.*

⋏ *After a flood, citizens are evacuated from the town of Mestia.*

⋎ *In Artvin, the population is equally divided between Muslims and Armenian Christians.*

➤ *At the Black Sea resort of Yalta,*
Stalin met with other Allied wartime
leaders in 1945.

⌄ *Givi Kandarely, a Georgian artist,*
stands before a painting that depicts
Georgian peasant life.

(continued from page 48)

In February 1921, riots broke out between the Bolsheviks and the Georgian army. The Bolsheviks appealed to their party leaders in Moscow for help. On February 16, the Red Army crossed the border from Azerbaijan. Nine days later they had taken Tbilisi. By March 18, the Bolsheviks were in control, answering to the Communist regime that controlled Russia.

Georgia's problems continued. In the following summer, a cholera outbreak killed thousands of people, and famine claimed countless more lives. These disasters weakened Georgia even further.

The Bolsheviks ended Georgia's claim to self-government in 1922 when they incorporated Georgia, Armenia, and Azerbaijan into the Transcaucasian Soviet Federated Socialist Republic and made it part of the Union of Soviet Socialist Republics. A period of severe repression began, aimed at Georgians who continued to resist Soviet control. An underground resistance movement formed in 1922, but many of its sympathizers and organizers were jailed or shot. The head of the Georgian church was jailed after calling on Western nations to help remove the Bolsheviks from power in Georgia. He later died in prison. In 1924, the the underground movement staged a rebellion, but the Red Army quickly defeated it.

With this victory, the Soviets finally established full control over Georgia. On December 5, 1936, the Transcaucasian Soviet Federated Socialist Republic was dissolved into three republics. Georgia became the Georgian Soviet Socialist Republic.

Georgian native Joseph Stalin (right) is shown vacationing in 1922 at Gorky in Russia with Vladimir Lenin.

Georgia under
the Soviets

When the Communists came to power in Georgia in 1921, they put
into effect a plan with three major parts: industrialization, central-
ization of agriculture, and cultural revolution. With this plan, the
Soviets have succeeded in transforming Georgia into a modern industrial society.

Modernization has caused changes in life-style for many Georgians. Traditional dress has largely given way to European clothing,
and life among the workers in the cities is much like that throughout
the rest of the Soviet Union. In the countryside, the Soviets have
replaced the small family farms and the estates of the nobility with
large government-run farms that require modern machinery and
many workers.

Virtually all aspects of Georgian life—where and how the people
live and work, what types of industry are developed, what goods are
available in shops and at what prices, and so on—are controlled by
the government. The government is also responsible for making
health care and housing available to everyone.

The government of Soviet Georgia is modeled on the central
government in Moscow. Soviets (councils) from the towns and villages form the basic unit of government and are responsible for local

affairs. Representatives from the soviets form the 440-member Georgian Supreme Soviet, the highest governing body in the republic. The Georgian Supreme Soviet is elected for four years from a single list of candidates; voters endorse or strike out the candidates' names as desired. As one of the republics of the USSR, Georgia also sends representatives to the Supreme Soviet of the USSR.

Georgia also contains two autonomous soviet socialist republics (ASSRs) and one autonomous oblast (region) within its borders. The autonomous republics have their own capitals, local governments, school systems, and newspapers. The autonomous republics and oblast are the result of the early Communist decision to allow ethnic minorities in the Soviet Union some control over local affairs in "homeland" areas. For example, the Adzharian ASSR is home to the Muslim Georgians, who have always resisted domination by the Christian majority. In addition to the Adzharian ASSR (whose capital is Batumi), Georgia also includes the Abkhazian ASSR (whose capital is Sukhumi) and the South Ossetian Autonomous Oblast (whose capital is Tskhinvali).

Although the Supreme Soviet theoretically governs the country, true power in Georgia and the Soviet Union resides in the Communist party. It is the only political party permitted in the USSR and membership is selective. In fact, only about 6 percent of Soviet citizens belong to the party because admission is difficult and time-consuming. Important government posts are always held by influential party members, who are required to follow party directives. The Communist party, headquartered in Moscow, controls the Georgian government through the head of the Communist party in Georgia.

But the party's power does not mean that the government is useless. Rather, the government is necessary for the party to put its policies into effect. In other words, the party makes the decisions, and the government carries them out. To Westerners, the official

The current leader of the U.S.S.R. is Mikhail Gorbachev, General Secretary of the Communist party.

government may seem to be the puppet of the political party. But the people of the Soviet Union do not see it this way. They make no attempt to hide the fact that the party—as the voice of the working class—is firmly in charge.

The basic party unit is the primary party organization (formally called "cells"), a group that has from three to several thousand members. Primary party organizations may be formed in a factory, farm, village, military unit, university, or anywhere that people live or work. The primary party organizations are supervised by a district party office. The district party offices are, in turn, ultimately under the control of the republic committee.

Every three to five years, selected party members from all over the Soviet Union meet for a party congress. The party congress elects the Central Committee, whose members direct the party. The Central Committee includes the Politburo (short for Political Bureau), the body that makes policy decisions for the party. The general secretary heads the Politburo (and the entire party) and is the most powerful person in the USSR. Mikhail S. Gorbachev currently holds that position.

Georgia's Educational System

Education has always been important to the Georgians. The Colchis Academy, founded in the 4th century A.D., was modeled on the Greek Academy of Aristotle. In later centuries, the Georgian church ran the schools and seminaries that provided Georgia with an educated class.

Soon after they came to power, the Soviets decided to eliminate illiteracy in Georgia. They placed the schools, most of which had been run by the church, under state control, and started teaching classes in Russian rather than in Georgian. By 1930, this form of education was required for all school-age children in the country.

Today, Georgian students must go to school for at least eight years. About 78,000 teachers work with more than a million students in more than 4,500 general-education schools throughout the republic. After a Georgian student finishes this basic education, he or she can go to one of the more than 100 secondary schools. Each of

Karl Marx's teachings form the core of Soviet education.

these schools specializes in a specific area of study, such as agriculture, education, medicine, economics, or finance.

After secondary school, a student may attend a professional or technical school for training in any of 180 specialties, or he or she may attend one of the 19 colleges and universities in Georgia. These institutions include the University of Tbilisi, the V.I. Lenin Georgian Polytechnical Institute, the Academy of Arts, eight institutes for teacher training, three agricultural institutes, a medical school, a veterinary school, a theater institute, a music conservatory, and a physical-education institute.

The largest Georgian college, the University of Tbilisi, was founded after the Russian Revolution in 1917. It includes the Academy of Sciences, where researchers study computer science, physics, earthquake-proof construction methods, machine science, and robotics. At the academy, some researchers are trying to create a machine that will automatically translate spoken Russian into Georgian. Others are developing new drugs from native Georgian plants. Still others are studying paleontology, biology, botany, and physiology.

In the tradition of the ancient Colchis Academy, the University of Tbilisi has an Institute of Philosophy, which instructs students in what Westerners call political science. In Georgia and throughout the USSR, the doctrines of Marx and Lenin dominate the study of philosophy.

Health Care

Like education, health care is run exclusively by the government in Georgia. The republic has more than 500 hospitals and nearly 2,000 dispensaries and clinics. It also has more than 17,000 doctors—about 1 for every 300 people. Georgia's therapeutic mineral springs and health spas on the Black Sea have helped earn the republic a reputation as a health-care center.

At some collective farms, tea picking has been mechanized.

The Georgian Economy

In a little more than 50 years of Soviet government, Georgia has made enormous economic progress. Its simple rural way of life has largely given way to modern factories, mills, farms, resorts, and power stations. Today, Georgia is one of the most prosperous republics of the Soviet Union.

Georgia is a major source of raw manufacturing materials for the Soviet Union. Its northwestern mountains yield coal, and the region near Kutaisi is one of the world's richest sources of manganese, a mineral used to make high-grade steel.

Georgia's major industrial center is Rustavi, about 20 miles (32 kilometers) southeast of Tbilisi. Rustavi houses an iron and steel mill and chemical plants. The laminated sheet iron and seamless pipe products produced at Rustavi are used throughout the Soviet Union. The chemical plants in Rustavi produce fertilizers, synthetic materials, and medications.

Throughout Georgia modern factories make such diverse products as heavy farm equipment, locomotives, and tea-gathering machines. Light industries produce cotton, wool, and silk and have largely eliminated the need for importing these items. Georgia's food-processing industry produces tea, dairy products, and canned goods. Tobacco-processing is also an important industry. Georgia leads the USSR in the production of table and dessert wines.

Essential to Georgian industry are the country's fast-flowing rivers, which provide an abundant source of energy. More than 200 hydroelectric dams have been built to tap the energy of the Rioni, Kura, and other Georgian rivers.

Industrial production accounts for nearly three-fifths of Georgia's income. Agriculture also plays a major role in Georgia's economy, providing more than one-fifth of the republic's income. Construction, transportation, communications, commerce, services, and tourism account for the remainder.

With its warm days and plentiful rainfall—up to 100 inches (254 millimeters) a year—Georgia's coastal region is the most fertile land in the Soviet Union. But in the rest of Georgia, farmland is in short supply and difficult to work because of the mountainous terrain. To compensate, the Georgians grow highly profitable crops, such as tea and citrus fruits.

On the coast, farms also grow corn, sugar beets, melons, vegetables, wine grapes, olives, figs, persimmons, pomegranates, loquats, and tobacco. Plants such as geraniums, roses, sorghum, jasmine, and basil thrive here, too, and are used in the perfume industry. Lumber is another important commodity, especially that from exotic trees, such as eucalyptus and bamboo.

In the mountains, the climate favors crops such as barley, oats, peaches, apples, cherries, apricots, and plums. Shepherds tend sheep and goats in the mountain pastures. The warm, dry countryside around Tbilisi is ideal for growing grapes, and the region is famous for its wine. Large irrigation projects have also made it possible to grow other crops, such as winter wheat.

The traditional concept of owning and working a farm has changed dramatically under Soviet rule. It has been replaced by a system of collective and state farms. The collective farm, or *kolkhoz*,

Men and women of all ages work to harvest leaves at a tea plantation near Batumi.

is a cooperative organization in which a group of people pool their livestock and farm machinery and work together on land leased from the government. The collective farm must meet a production quota and its profits are generally distributed on the basis of the number of workdays contributed by each member.

Weak or unprofitable collectives are merged into other collectives or turned into state farms, or sovkhoz. The government owns and operates these farms, providing modern equipment and paying the workers regular wages. Although the state farm is the Com-

This newly renovated plant is scheduled to produce thousands of heavy trucks that will be used to make Soviet farms more efficient and productive.

munist ideal, it is expensive to run because the state must pay wages year-round.

In 1984, 696 collective farms held more than 66 percent of Georgia's farmland and 546 state farms held most of the rest. Garden plots owned by individuals are allowed on the collective farms, and even though they make up only a small amount of the total land farmed, they produce as much as 40 percent of Georgia's entire agricultural output, according to some estimates.

Tourist Resorts

Aided by improved transportation, tourism is a growing part of the Georgian economy. The Black Sea coast is famous for its health spas, and the balmy weather and sandy beaches make it a popular vacation area for people throughout the Soviet Union.

Tourists from outside the Soviet Union are becoming increasingly common. Vacationers in Georgia are also attracted to the cool, clear air of the Caucasus Mountains. At the resorts north of Batumi, visitors can enjoy skiing, mountain climbing, swimming, or relaxing in the wild, scenic peaks of the Caucasus.

Tbilisi is set against the backdrop of the rugged terrain common throughout Georgia.

In the Cities and Villages

Nowhere in Georgia is the contrast between old and new so visible as in its cities and towns. In the urban areas, ancient palaces and temples stand beside modern high-rise apartments and Soviet monuments. Old buildings that once housed the offices of princes and tsars now serve the Soviet government. A modern subway system runs beneath the streets of Tbilisi.

The modernization of Georgia has made its cities and towns more important. With the shift toward industry and increased education, many Georgians have left the hard life of the rural villages for the cities. With them have come problems, especially a shortage of housing. Despite the government's extensive building programs, many large families must still crowd into small apartments.

But even with the crowding, urban Georgia offers a life-style as good as or better than that of any other part of the USSR. The inhabitants enjoy balmy weather, beautiful parks, and clean streets, as well as theaters, museums, cultural centers, and educational institutions. And the resorts and beaches of the coastal cities attract tourists from throughout the Soviet Union and beyond.

Georgia's major cities include Tbilisi, the capital; Sukhumi and Batumi on the Black Sea coast; Kutaisi in the mining region; and

Rustavi, the site of Georgia's major industries. Each of these cities is important to the region's history and culture, and each offers a unique view of Georgian life today.

Tbilisi

Georgia's capital city is home to more than a million people. It stretches for 28 miles (49 kilometers) along the high bluffs overlooking the Kura River, but it is only 4.5 miles (7.2 km) wide. Elegant gardens line the banks of the Kura, which is overlooked by Metekhi Cathedral, one of the city's best-known landmarks. A large statue of Mother Georgia also overlooks the Kura. She holds a sword in one hand and extends a cup of wine in the other—the symbols of Georgian nationalism and traditional hospitality.

Tbilisi was founded 1,500 years ago during the reign of King Vakhtang Gorgaslani. According to legend, the king wounded a deer while hunting in the area, which fell into a hot sulfur spring along the Kura River. It emerged from the spring recovered from its wound.

Although it is far from the sea, Tbilisi looks and feels like a coastal Mediterranean city. It is hilly, with an average elevation of more than 1,200 feet (364 meters), and is surrounded by mountains. Tile-roofed houses with ornate painted balconies climb the steep slopes beneath Zion Temple, the ancient fortress that dominates the Tbilisi skyline. The narrow streets and open air markets of Old Tbilisi are full of exotic sights and smells, as merchants of half a dozen nationalities sell food and flowers.

At the center of Old Tbilisi is Irakly Square. Formerly known as Royal Square, officials of the Georgian kings used to stand in the square and settle disputes, listen to the people's complaints, and make royal proclamations. During Georgia's colonial period, the government used the square in a similar way. In fact, the old Governor's Palace (now the police headquarters) faces the square. The Cathedral

The Polytechnical Institute is one of the more impressive buildings in Tbilisi.

of the Assumption, one of the largest and oldest churches in Tbilisi, stands close by. Parts of the original structure date to around 600 A.D., but most of it was rebuilt in the 19th century.

Lenin Square has replaced Irakly Square as the hub of city life. The Georgian Art Museum stands at one side of the square and exhibits samples of ancient and modern Georgian metalwork, painting, and sculpture. In colonial days, the museum building housed the Tbilisi Ecclesiastical Seminary, a religious boarding school attended by Soviet dictator Joseph Stalin from 1894 to 1899.

From Lenin Square, one can travel through the city along Rustaveli Boulevard to Rustaveli Square. The boulevard and the square are named after Georgia's greatest poet, Shota Rustaveli, who lived in the 12th century. Shaded by large sycamore trees and lined with museums, theaters, hotels, and government offices, Rustaveli Boulevard is a popular place for an evening stroll.

Not far away is the University of Tbilisi and Victory Park. The park has 300 acres (121 hectares) of fountains, shady walkways, open-air cinemas, and cafes. Ordzhonikidze Park, a few miles away, also contains an open-air cinema, a theater, a parachute tower, and a planetarium.

The highest point in Tbilisi is Mount Mtatsminda, which can be reached by cable car. A restaurant and park are at the mountain's peak, and a large botanical garden covers its slopes.

Sukhumi

Sukhumi is the capital of the Abkhazian ASSR (Abkhazia). It has a population of 122,000, and lies on Georgia's northwest coast along Sukhumi Bay. Sukhumi's climate is subtropical, much like that of the coast of Spain. Spring comes in February, and the weather is warm from April until November.

According to legend, Sukhumi was founded by the Greeks in the 5th or 6th century B.C. Known in ancient times as Dioscurias, this city was an important trading center on the Black Sea. To defend the city from raiders and invaders, the people of Sukhumi built a fort on the city's harbor. For protection on the landward side, the city built the Great Abkhazian Wall, a system of interconnected forts that stretched for 100 miles (160 kilometers) between the Kelasura and Mokvi rivers. Most of these forts still stand today. Sukhumi also contains many other ruins of ancient temples, churches, and bridges.

Today, people come to Sukhumi to relax. Its climate makes it a popular site for health spas, and for people who suffer from heart and lung disease. A tuberculosis sanatorium is 6 miles (9.6 kilometers) away at Gulripsi. Besides the spas, Sukhumi also houses leather and tobacco factories as well as shipyards and canneries. As the capital of Abkhazia, it also serves as an important governmental center.

Along the seafront, Sukhumi's old bazaars have been replaced by parks and gardens full of exotic plants, such as camphor trees, palms, and cedars, and numerous fountains and monuments. Sukhumi's botanical gardens were founded in 1840 and contain more than 800 plant species, including a plant that flowers for a single day each year. Eucalyptus trees fill the city. The trees were introduced into Georgia by 19th-century Australian trading ships, which originally carried the seeds as ballast.

Trapetsia Mountain looms just outside of Sukhumi. A colony of about 2,000 monkeys lives in a park on the mountain. The monkeys are used for medical research at the Institute of Medical Biology.

Batumi

Batumi, the capital of the Adzharian ASSR (Adzharia), lies in the southwest corner of Georgia, just 12 miles (19 kilometers) from the Turkish border. Well known for its oil refineries and its busy harbor, Batumi is connected by pipeline with the oilfields of Baku on the Caspian Sea in Azerbaijan. Batumi, an important Georgian port city with a population of 129,000, exports oil, tea, and canned goods.

Batumi's weather is even warmer and more tropical than that of Sukhumi. An extremely clean city, most of its houses and buildings are a brilliant white, and the streets are virtually spotless. Like Sukhumi, it is a popular resort as well as a seaport.

Kutaisi and Rustavi

Kutaisi lies between Tbilisi and Sukhumi in the Rioni River Valley. In ancient times, the city was known as the capital of Colchis, the land where Jason and the Argonauts sought the Golden Fleece. In medieval times it was the capital of Imeretia, one of Georgia's small principalities. Today, it is a thriving modern city of about 207,000 people, a center of government, and home to the country's textile and mining industries.

A symbol of the new, industrialized Georgia, Rustavi was built after World War II on the site of an ancient village. Most of Rustavi's 139,000 inhabitants work in its vast mining and manufacturing complex. But Rustavi is more than a large factory town. It has its own museum and, like most Georgian cities, its own theaters, cinemas, and dance companies.

Away from Georgia's major cities, progress has come to smaller towns and villages as well. Much of Georgia's rural population actually works in the factories and businesses of nearby cities. Villages now have factories that process agricultural products, ore, and light industrial products. These enterprises have changed the slow-paced traditional villages into modern communities.

As in the urban areas, modern buildings coexist with ancient buildings. Remote mountain towns now have electricity, roads, schools, hospitals, and hotels. But many people still live in old stone houses with battle towers that were once stocked with provisions and ammunition in order to withstand sieges by invading armies.

Getting Around in Georgia

Tucked among the southern slopes of the Caucasus is a remote valley called Svanetia—a word that means "shelter" or "refuge." According to local legend, fugitives would flee to Svanetia to escape the authorities. The steep mountains surrounding Svanetia made it accessible only to those traveling by foot. In the winter months, snow cut off Svanetia completely from the outside world. Any policeman or soldier who made his way into the valley would then have to face the proud Svan warriors, who recognized no authority but their own and who pledged that they would fight and die rather than turn over a fugitive. Even the most dedicated government servants were un-

The Transcaucasian Highway will carry traffic all year long and provide access to most regions of Soviet Georgia.

willing to follow a suspect who had found his way to the valley of the Svans.

Today, a road carries travelers into Svanetia. But the 81-mile (130-kilometer) trip from the nearest town, Zugdidi, takes nine hours of tortuous driving. And this trip becomes impossible in winter months, when snow and ice make Svanetia accessible only by airplane.

Even in more accessible regions of Georgia, travel can be difficult. The same mountains that isolate Soviet Georgia from its neighbors also break the republic's people into small, independent groups who traditionally have had little contact with one another. Georgia's modern roads, railroads, and airports link its major cities to each other and to the outside world, but its mountainous terrain continues to complicate travel to and from the smaller towns and villages.

Georgia has about 20,930 miles (33,700 kilometers) of roads. About 18,570 miles (29,900 km) of them are paved. Georgia's largest and most important highway, the Georgian military highway, owes its very existence to isolated regions such as Svanetia. When the Imperial Russian army came to Georgia in the 1800s, it expected to bring the independent mountain people under control. But like earlier conquerors, the Russian army found its soldiers stuck in the cities with no way to move around the country. So the Russians constructed the Georgian military highway, which crosses the spine of the Caucasus Mountains and links Tbilisi with the Russian Soviet Socialist Republic (Russia). The highway begins in the city of Ordzhonikidze in Russia and twists and turns for 130 miles (208 km) through high passes and tunnels until it reaches Tbilisi. The Russians also built highways from Ordzhonikidze to Kutaisi and from Sukhumi to Cherkessk.

Although these roads are more than a century old, they are still the most important highways in Georgia. But during the winter months, snow and ice close down the Georgian military highway, and travelers from the north must enter Georgia by way of the Black Sea. To solve this problem, a new highway is under construction and a long tunnel cuts beneath the highest mountains to permit year-round travel.

Rugged terrain prohibits rail lines from crossing the Caucasus. But rail passengers and freight can reach Georgia by the main line that runs along the Black Sea coast to Sukhumi. From Sukhumi, the railroad runs east to Tbilisi and on to Baku in Azerbaijan. Another line runs south from Sukhumi to Batumi. These lines connect with many spurs to outlying regions and smaller towns. A total of about 915 miles (1,430 kilometers) of rail line exists. The trains carry 50 to 100 million tons (56 to 111 million metric tons) of freight and more than 22 million passengers a year.

Georgia's transportation system also includes major seaports at Batumi, Poti, and Sukhumi. Batumi serves as the end of a pipeline from the oilfields of Baku and as an important outlet for oil and petroleum products.

Transportation improvements in recent decades have helped to connect Georgia with the outside world and to bring it into the 20th century. Indeed, Georgia is now just a short flight from Moscow and Istanbul. Instead of climbing treacherous mountain passes, modern travelers can fly over them and look down on the land of the proud Georgians.

Georgian craftsmen are noted for the intricacy of their designs in metalwork.

Georgian Arts
and Culture

In October 1986, the Soviet government announced that it would release a Georgian film about the reign of terror under the dictator Joseph Stalin. This was a surprising announcement because the Soviet government has almost totally ignored the Stalin era—a time of mass arrests, deportations, and executions. Since the late 1950s, the average citizen has heard almost nothing from official sources about Stalin or his rule. Under General Secretary Mikhail Gorbachev, however, the Soviet government has allowed artists more freedom to tackle such controversial subjects.

The film *Repentance* tells the story of Varlim Aravidze, the dictator of a fictional Georgian city. This character is modeled on Lavrenti Beria, a Georgian native who served as Stalin's chief of secret police for many years. In the film, Aravidze grows increasingly cruel and bizarre, and at one point rounds up all of the city's inhabitants who have a certain last name. The film shows the terror of the prisons and secret police under Stalin's reign, subjects that have been ignored in official Soviet history books.

The film was conceived, produced, and filmed in Soviet Georgia, and directed by a Georgian, Tengiz Abuladze. He completed the film in 1984, but at that time the government would not allow its release.

Film director Tengiz Abuladze's recent motion picture Repentance *examines Soviet life under Stalin.*

Abuladze's subject matter was no surprise to those familiar with the Soviet film industry. In the arts, as in other areas of Soviet life, Georgia has a reputation for being more colorful, more liberal, and more daring than the rest of the Soviet Union.

Throughout the USSR, the role of the arts is very different than it is in Western countries. In the West, funding for the arts is often scarce, and many artists find it difficult to support themselves. In the USSR, however, government funding supports painting, theater, literature, and other artistic disciplines, which makes it possible even for young, unknown artists to work in their chosen fields.

But in return for this funding, the government expects the artists to support—or at least not to criticize—the Communist party's political beliefs. In fact, the government believes that the arts should reinforce the Soviet view of life.

Although the state does not physically control the arts, it influences them through unwritten rules. Artists know, for example, that the government favors certain themes and will provide more money for them. That is why Socialist Realism—a style favored by the Soviet government—is common throughout the USSR. Socialist Realism stresses patriotism and easily understood subject matter. But now that the official view of acceptable art is changing, other styles and topics are beginning to emerge. Not surprisingly, Georgia is leading the way.

Although Moscow and Leningrad are considered to be the traditional cultural centers of the USSR, cultural life tends to be more dynamic and innovative in the outlying republics, where politics are less intrusive. Georgians are especially proud of their artistic heritage and support it enthusiastically. This is especially evident in the number of amateur theatrical groups, dance groups, choral groups, drama groups, musical ensembles, folk theaters, libraries, and museums in Georgia.

Georgian children who show artistic potential attend special art schools. They can go on to secondary schools, which qualify them to teach art, or they can enter a six-year diploma program. After their schooling, they can apply for jobs directly through the Artist's Union.

Irakli Ochiauri, a sculptor, painter, and metalworker, has commented on the unique place of Georgian art within the USSR. He says that Georgian art is "more mannered and stylized" than other types of art, meaning that it features certain highly recognizable elements. For example, Georgian sculpture tends to show elongated faces with masklike features.

Georgian artists have excelled in metalwork, sculpture, and other arts for centuries. Georgia was famous throughout the ancient world for its jewelry and other luxury metal items. Excavations in Trialeti have uncovered many fine examples of metalwork, including a filigreed (etched) gold cup set with gems, dating back to 2000 B.C.

The introduction of Christianity brought great advances in painting, church architecture, and sculpture. Early Georgian Christians were highly skilled in enameling, wood-carving, and fresco painting (painting with watercolors on wet plaster). Two master artists, Beka Opizari and Beshken Opizara, flourished in the late 12th

The Georgian Museum in Tiflis houses a vast collection of arts, crafts, and other items showing the region's culture.

century. One of them created the famous Khakuli icon (an icon is a religious image painted on a small panel often beautifully orna-mented). The Khakuli icon consists of a 10th century enameled por-trait of the Virgin Mary surrounded by gold filigree and precious gems.

The Georgian Theater

The performing arts in Georgia also have a rich and ancient tradition. Georgians have attended plays at least since the 5th century B.C. In modern-day Georgia, the theater still thrives; nearly every town and village has a theater company.

During International Theatre Day Georgians perform Shakespeare's Richard III.

One of the foremost directors in Georgian theater is Mikhail Tumanishvili. Greatly influenced by the horrors of World War II, his work has shaken up the Georgian theater. In the 1950s, he was accused of rejecting the traditions of the theater, and of distorting the classics. But times have changed. Tumanishvili and his colleagues now hold the titles of Merited or People's Artists.

The "Simel," a folklore group in southern Ossetia, performs in an outdoor concert.

Motion Pictures

The Russian Communist party leader Lenin once said, "Of all the arts, for us, cinema is the most important." Soviet film attendance proves this statement to be true: the average Soviet citizen goes to the movies 23 times a year.

In the USSR, the government controls all aspects of filmmaking—production, distribution, and exhibition. A night at the movies

usually consists of three parts. The first part is *Novosti dyna* (News of the Day), which may feature information on party functions, industry progress, agriculture, or the space program. News is rarely negative unless a moral lesson can be drawn from the story. The second part is a short film, which is basically more propaganda. Finally, a full-length feature film is shown. The themes of these films tend to be socialistic and patriotic.

In Georgia, feature films are made at the Gruziia film studio. Many are filmed in the local language and reflect local cultural traditions. The first Georgian movie was a documentary filmed between 1908 and 1910. Topics of recent Georgian films have included the fall of Berlin in World War II and heroic figures of Georgian history.

Song and Dance

Georgians have been composing, singing, and dancing for centuries. Traditional song and dance is still a part of everyday life. For example, ancient Georgians performed the dance of the hunt in honor of the moon, which was believed to be the god of fertility. Today, Georgian men still perform the *fundruki*, a dance done on the tips of the toes and based on this ancient dance.

In addition to the many traditional folk dance ensembles, Georgians have enjoyed and supported ballet since their first ballet company was formed in 1852. Outside the republic, many other people appreciate Georgian dance. In 1959, the Georgian State Dance Company performed in London. The British press praised "these men with fire in their feet" and wrote of "the company's tall dark-eyed women . . . who behaved as though they loved dancing only slightly less than they admired the decorous chivalry of their nimble-footed gallants."

The earliest evidence of Georgian music dates from the 8th century B.C., when choral groups used rich harmonies in ancient Georgian songs. These songs were handed down for many years. In the 4th century A.D., the spread of Christianity caused Georgian church music to develop. In the 19th century, the annexation of Georgia to Russia broadened Georgia's musical boundaries beyond traditional songs and dances. By 1851, an opera house had opened in Tbilisi. Twenty years later, music schools sprang up. In 1885, Lado Agniashvili organized the first Georgian national choir. The

Georgian Philharmonic Society was set up in 1905, and the Society of Young Georgian Musicians, which includes a symphony orchestra and a string quartet, was founded in 1922.

As a result of its rich heritage, Georgia has all types of music and dance. It even has yearly pop music festivals where thousands of Soviet "hippies" gather. And in Abkhazia, there is a troupe of singers and dancers that is composed entirely of centenarians.

An unusual Georgian "art" is wrestling. Part sport and part dance, traditional Georgian wrestling resembles judo. It is unusual because the wrestlers are not permitted to use chokeholds or to fight while lying down; it is unique among wrestling forms in that the contestants wrestle to music.

Literature

The Georgian language belongs to the Caucasian language group family, which makes it quite distinct from most European and Central Asian languages. The dialects of most remote Georgian regions are well defined and similar to the standard Georgian spoken in the cities. But the Svanians and Mingrelo-Laz speak entirely different languages. All dialects of Georgian have extremely complicated verb structures. Because foreigners find the region's languages difficult to master, very little is known about Georgian literature outside the republic.

Before the Georgian language was written down, many myths, legends, fairy tales, poems, and proverbs were handed down verbally or written in Greek or Persian. The conversion of the Georgians to Christianity in the 4th century gave rise to a written language and consequently to Georgian literature. The church needed an alphabet and a written language to help spread religious teachings. Literacy grew, and by the 5th century, the first Georgian literature was being written. Early works included translations of the Bible and accounts

Maxim Gorky, one of Russia's most popular novelists, arrives in Moscow.

of the lives of the saints. The first writing style was an angular form known as *khutsuri* (ecclesiastic) because it was used for church writings.

Church writings dominated literature until the end of the 11th century. By that time, a flowing, rounded writing style called *mkhedruli* (knightly) had evolved for laymen. Contact with Persian literature influenced Georgian writers and ushered in the Golden Age of Georgian literature. Historical accounts appeared during the Middle Ages, under the title of *Kartlis Tskhovreba* (The Life of Georgia). Georgians also began to write heroic tales, novels, and epic poems. The most famous was Shota Rustaveli's *The Knight in the Tiger's Skin,* an epic poem using the Georgian themes of bravery, hospitality, and national pride.

In the following centuries, literary themes changed with the times. The struggle for liberation prevailed in Georgian literature of the 17th and 18th centuries. In the 19th century, under the influence of the Western literary world, Romanticism (a literary and artistic movement stressing the goodness of nature and the expression of individual emotions) was introduced to Soviet Georgia. The work of the novelist and poet Ilia Chavchavadze strongly promoted this theme.

Romanticism gave way to realism (the use of common language and scenes set in everyday life) in the second half of the 19th century, as Georgian writers began to concentrate on the problems of class struggle and social reconstruction. During this time a young Russian writer named Maxim Gorky published his first story in a local Tbilisi paper. He later became one of the Soviet Union's leading literary figures. His books have been published throughout the world in many languages.

This photo depicts a hilltop fortress built by the ancient Persians in the old city of Tiflis.

A Balancing Act

Soviet Georgia is a land balanced between the past and the future. In remote mountain villages, life goes on as it has for centuries. Shepherds and their families live in simple cottages without electricity. These mountain people are virtually cut off from the outside world. Yet in Georgia's cities, cars clog modern streets, factories produce trucks, airplanes, and farm machinery, and scientists pursue the latest advances in physics and astronomy.

The republic is also geographically balanced between Russia to the north and Turkey to the south. It lies just across the Black Sea from the western edge of Europe. For centuries, Georgia's strategic location and natural resources have made it attractive to conquering nations. Its many neighbors have influenced Georgia, but the republic has managed to keep its uniqueness.

Within its borders, Georgia balances the interests of its varied inhabitants. The republic contains autonomous republics and regions, and more than 15 major ethnic groups, including such diverse peoples as Armenians, Russians, and Ossetians. Georgia's population also includes Christians, Muslims, and Jews who work in many different occupations and live in cities, towns, and remote rural areas. Despite their diversity, the people of Georgia live in harmony.

An ambitious construction program has provided much-needed living quarters to thousands of Georgian families.

Soviet Georgians are balanced between political worlds. Although they live in a Communist republic where the government controls the production and distribution of goods, they take great pride in their reputation as traders and dealers. They seem to enjoy the fact that they can bend the rules of the Soviet system so well. Although they owe their allegiance to Moscow, they have a reputation for being independent thinkers and fierce warriors.

What does the future hold for Soviet Georgia? How will it maintain its balancing act? As in the past, its fate will be bound to that of the USSR's. And as in the past, Georgians will work to maintain their independent identity. After all, Georgians are not Russians. They have their own language, their own traditions, and their own way of doing things—and they show no signs of changing. Several other factors will help them retain their Georgian identity. The ties that bind Georgia to Moscow will probably always be weaker than those of the other republics because Georgia was one of the last republics to be made a part of the Soviet Union. In addition, the recent easing of government policy toward the arts should allow Georgians greater freedom to develop and express their independent feelings.

Under Soviet rule, Georgia has become one of the most prosperous regions in the USSR. In the future, Georgia is likely to continue its economic progress, but its resources will have to be handled properly. Georgia's fertile lands will need to be farmed wisely in order to conserve farmland. The housing shortage will have to be solved in order to accommodate the growing number of people moving to the cities. And more roads will be needed to move Georgia's people and goods.

Whatever the future holds, the Georgians will find a way to make the best of it. Although the sword has passed over their land countless times, the image endures of a large, colorful family seated at the banquet table with their goblets raised for the final toast of the evening: "To Georgia! To Life!"

◄ G L O S S A R Y ►

Aul	A village.
Blat	A term that encompasses all of the methods— from patronage to fraud—used to bend Soviet rules.
Bolshevik	Russian for "majority." This term applies to the more radical members of the Social Democratic party. The Bolsheviks eventually gained control of the Russian government and renamed the Social Democratic party the Communist party.
Burkah	A cape worn as part of traditional Georgian dress.
Cell	The basic unit of the Communist party in the Soviet Union.
Centenarian	A person 100 or more years old.
Cherkeska	The traditional knee-length tunic worn by Georgian men and women.
Fundruki	An ancient Georgian dance that is still performed.
Judeo-Tats	The "Mountain Jews," a group of Jews living in Georgia's mountain valleys.
Kartelebi	The Georgians' name for themselves.

Kefir — Liquid yogurt. Centenarians attribute their long lives in part to a good diet that includes kefir and other dairy products.

Kolkhoz — A cooperative organization in which the government leases land to farm members who pool their livestock and farm machinery. The collective farm is obligated to meet a delivery quota and divides profits among members, usually based on total workdays contributed.

Lenin — Vladimir Ilyich Lenin, leader of the Bolsheviks. Lenin directed the 1917 Revolution and was head of the first Soviet government.

Marxism — The theory and practice of Socialism as advocated by Karl Marx. One of its basic principles is that the means of producing and distributing goods are owned and operated by the state rather than by private individuals. All members of the community are to share in the work and the products.

Menshevik — Russian for "minority." This term refers to members of the more moderate faction of the Social Democratic party.

Oblast — A region set aside for occupation by a distinct but small ethnic group.

Ozakom — The committee appointed to govern Georgia, Azerbaijan, and Armenia after the 1917 Revolution.

Party Congress — A meeting of Communist party members held every three to five years.

Politboro — Short for political bureau, the body that controls the Soviet Communist party, and thus, the USSR.

Primary party organization — The basic unit of the Communist party in the Soviet Union.

Proletariat — The working class.

Rtveli   The "Festival of the Grape Harvest," a traditional Georgian holiday.

Shashlyk   A Georgian dish of lamb and onions roasted on a skewer.

Soviets   Literally, councils. Also used as the name of the people who live in the Soviet Union.

Sovkhoz   Farms owned and operated by the state. Employees are paid wages by the state.

Stalin   Literally, "man of steel." Stalin was the revolutionary name taken by the Georgian Josef Dzhugashvili, the Soviet dictator who ruled from 1922 to 1953.

Sveti Tskhoveli   "Pillar of Life," the primary church of Georgian Orthodoxy, located in the former capital city of Mtskheta.

Tsar   The title of the leader of Imperial Russia.

White Russians   A collection of groups who opposed the Bolsheviks and their Communist ideas after World War I. Many of the White Russians wanted to return to tsarist rule.

PICTURE CREDITS

AP/Wide World Photos: pp. 18, 21, 30, 58; Bettmann Newsphotos: pp. 50–51 (below), 61, 62, 90; Eastfoto: p. 2; Burt Glinn/Magnum: p. 53 (above); Intourist: pp. 50, 86–87; Library of Congress: pp. 30, 40–41, 45, 51 (above), 54 (below), 55 (below), 67, 84; Metropolitan Museum of Art: pp. 34, 39; PAR/NYC: pp. 22–23, 56 (above), 70, 80, 92; Tass from Sovfoto: pp. 14, 16, 24, 49, 52 (above & below), 52–53 (above & below), 54 (below), 55 (above), 56 (below), 68, 73, 77, 82, 85, 94; United Nations: pp. 34, 64.

◄INDEX►